DISNEY LEARNING

STEAM
SCIENCE TECHNOLOGY ENGINEERING ART MATH

Disney
PRINCESS

W9-CQW-047

tHiNK iT OUT!

Addition, Subtraction, Geometry, and More!

JEREMIAH KARA

Written by Stefanie Mathewson
Illustrated by the Disney Storybook Art Team

Dear Parents:

Disney Learning's Think It Out! series invites children to think, wonder, and talk about math. The activities are designed to deepen mathematical understanding and help learners become confident problem solvers.

There are many ways to solve a problem. This book encourages children to use a variety of strategies in order to solve the problem at hand. Children need time and space to think, reason, and even struggle a bit to arrive at solutions using strategies that make sense to them.

To nurture your child's mathematical explorations, try asking these questions:

- **How are you thinking about this problem?**
- **Why do you think this might work?**
- **Is there another way you can think about this problem?**
- **Can you explain that to me?**

Talking through the problem together is an important part of the learning process. Listen, rather than tell what you know. Consider your child's ideas. Respond with a question to keep the conversation going.

Math is everywhere. Talking about these concepts helps children better understand the world around them. Enjoy the mathematical adventure!

Table of Contents

Pattern Power!

Abu found many gems in the Cave of Wonders. Let's arrange them in a pattern.

Pattern Unit

Show the pattern in three different ways. Repeat the pattern twice.

Letters:

ABBCABBC

Numbers:

12231223

Actions:

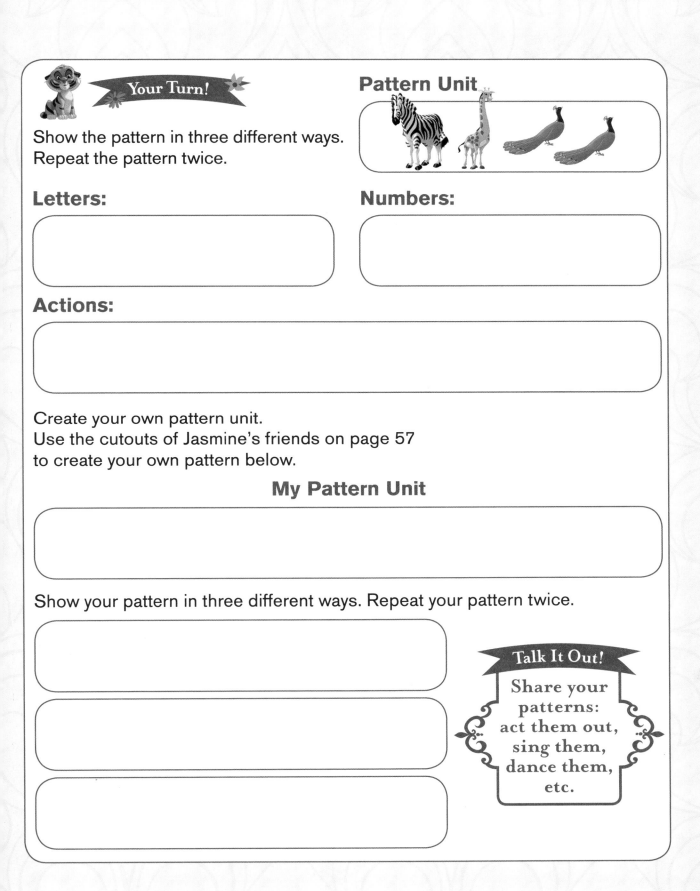

Your Turn!

Show the pattern in three different ways.
Repeat the pattern twice.

Pattern Unit

Letters:

Numbers:

Actions:

Create your own pattern unit.
Use the cutouts of Jasmine's friends on page 57
to create your own pattern below.

My Pattern Unit

Show your pattern in three different ways. Repeat your pattern twice.

Talk It Out!

Share your
patterns:
act them out,
sing them,
dance them,
etc.

Open Number Sentences

3 chipmunks are playing with Aurora.
Some are black and some are brown.
Color the chipmunks to show different ways to make 3.
Write an equation to match each combination.

Aurora's Friends	Chipmunks	Chipmunks	Equation
	3	0	3 + 0 = 3
	2	1	2 + 1 = 3
	1	2	1 + 2 = 3
	0	3	0 + 3 = 3

5 birds are listening to Aurora sing.
Some are blue and some are red.
Color the birds to show different ways to make 5.
Write an equation to match each combination.

Your Turn!

Birds	Equation
▽ ▽ ▽ ▽ ▽	
▽ ▽ ▽ ▽ ▽	
▽ ▽ ▽ ▽ ▽	
▽ ▽ ▽ ▽ ▽	
▽ ▽ ▽ ▽ ▽	
▽ ▽ ▽ ▽ ▽	

7 rabbits are with Aurora.
Some are gray and some are brown.
Color the rabbits to show different ways to make 7.
Write an equation to match each combination.

Rabbits	Equation
🐰🐰🐰🐰🐰🐰🐰	
🐰🐰🐰🐰🐰🐰🐰	
🐰🐰🐰🐰🐰🐰🐰	
🐰🐰🐰🐰🐰🐰🐰	
🐰🐰🐰🐰🐰🐰🐰	
🐰🐰🐰🐰🐰🐰🐰	
🐰🐰🐰🐰🐰🐰🐰	
🐰🐰🐰🐰🐰🐰🐰	

Talk It Out!
Share how you planned
your combinations.

Counting Fireflies with Tens and Ones

Ray and his family light up the bayou.
Let's count them.
Group 10 fireflies on a branch so they are easier to count.

10 ones are the same as 1 ten.

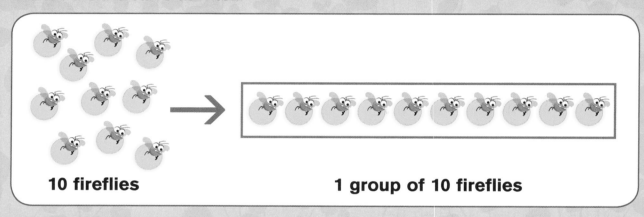

10 fireflies   **1 group of 10 fireflies**

Here are 26 fireflies.

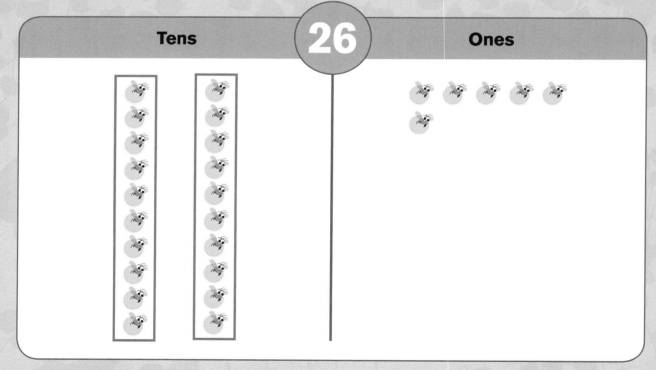

| Tens | 26 | Ones |

There are many fireflies in the night sky.
Use base ten blocks to count and show numbers
in more than one way.

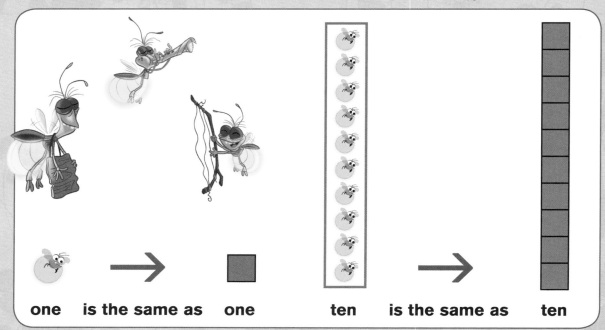

| one | is the same as | one | ten | is the same as | ten |

One way to make 33:

Another way to make 33:

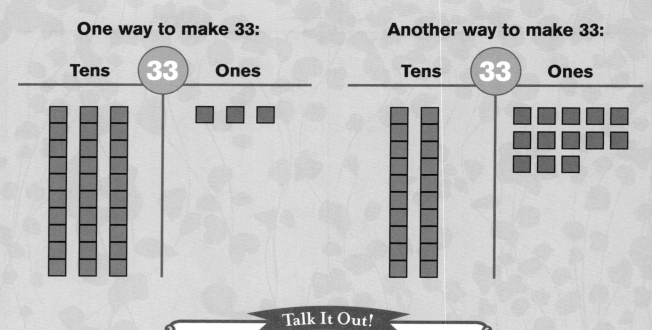

Tens **33** Ones

Tens **33** Ones

Talk It Out!

How are the 3s in 33 the same?
How are they different?

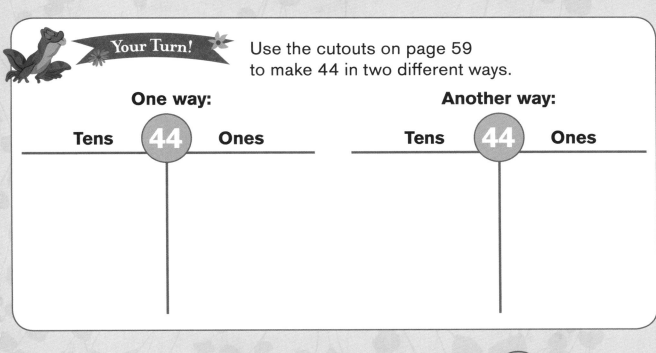

Use the cutouts on page 59 to make 44 in two different ways.

One way:

Tens ④④ Ones

Another way:

Tens ④④ Ones

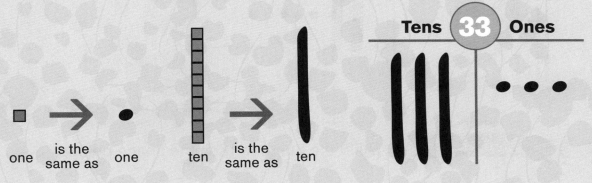

one → one   is the same as

ten → ten   is the same as

Tens ③③ Ones

Make 35 in two different ways. Draw the tens and ones.

One way:

Tens ③⑤ Ones

Another way:

Tens ③⑤ Ones

Building Numbers

Rapunzel likes adventures!
Go on a mathematical adventure.
Let's build numbers in different ways.
Build the number 25 in any way that makes sense to you.

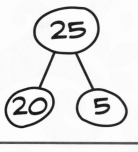

$$10 + 10 + 5 = 25$$

25

Your Turn!   Build the number 18 in the space below.

18

Pick a number to build in each space below.

19 | 27 31 48 55 64 73 82 96

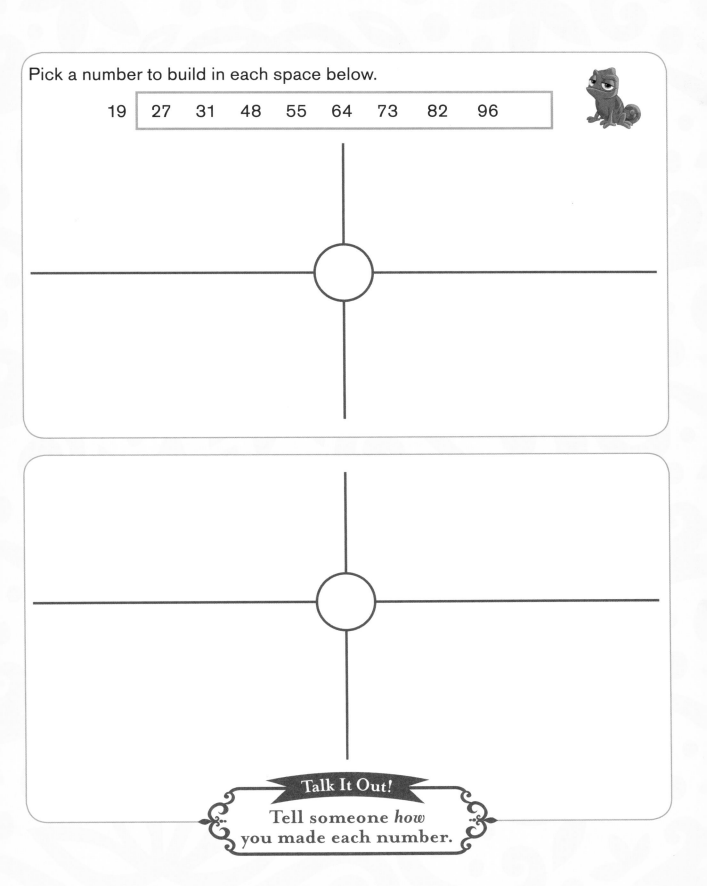

Talk It Out!

Tell someone *how* you made each number.

Solving Problems with Addition

Mulan has 17 fans.
She finds 19 more fans.
How many fans does Mulan have now?

One way:

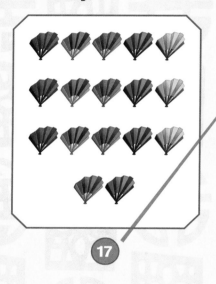

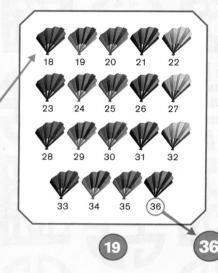

- Start at 17.
- Count 19 more.
- What number did you land on?

Another way:

0	1	2	3	4	5	6	7	8	9
10	11	12	13	14	15	16	(17) →18 ¹ →19 ²		
→20 ³ →21 ⁴ →22 ⁵ →23 ⁶ →24 ⁷ →25 ⁸ →26 ⁹ →27 ¹⁰ →28 ¹¹ →29 ¹²									
→30 ¹³ →31 ¹⁴ →32 ¹⁵ →33 ¹⁶ →34 ¹⁷ →35 ¹⁸ →(36) ¹⁹	37	38	39						
40	41	42	43	44	45	46	47	48	49

- Start at 17.
- Count 19 forward by ones.
- The number you land on is the answer.

Number sentence: 17 + 19 = 36
Mulan has a total of 36 fans.

Little Brother has ⬜ **bones.**

He finds ⬜ **more bones.**

How many bones does little brother have now?

Choose a number set.

(22 23) (42 53) (12 13) (72 63)

Circle the number set you want to use.

The numbers in each set are color-coded.

Place each number of the chosen set in the same-colored space in the problem.

Solve this problem in two ways that make sense to you.
Use pictures, numbers, or words.

One way: **Another way:**

Number sentence: _____

Little Brother has a total of _____ bones.

Talk It Out!

Share the strategy
you liked best and why.

©Disney

Attribute Arrows

Look at the arrowheads below.
How is each one different from the others and why?

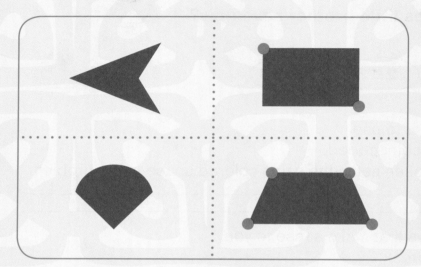

 This one is different because it has only two straight sides.
This one is different because it has one round part.

 This one is different because it has
3 sharp points.

 This one is different because it has
a red circle on every corner.

 This one is different because it has
two corners and two red circles.

Think of other ways the arrowheads are different from each other.

Look at the arrows below. How is each one different from the others and why?

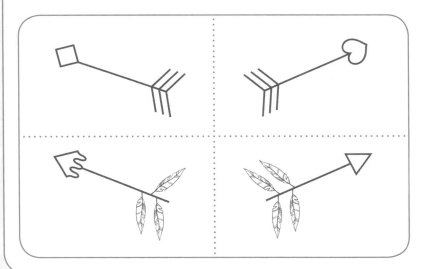

Look at the biscuits below. How is each one different from the others and why?

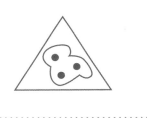

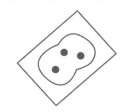

Talk It Out!

Ask your friends how they think the biscuits are different and why.

Muffin Multiplication

Snow White makes 3 muffins.
Each muffin has 2 berries on top.
How many berries are there altogether?

One way:

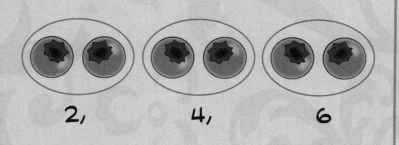

2,   4,   6

Another way:

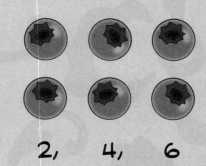

2,   4,   6

There are <u>6</u> berries altogether.

Snow White makes **muffins for the Dwarfs.**

Each muffin has **berries on top.**

How many berries are there altogether?

Choose a number set.

 4   5   **8   2**   **6   10**   **3   4**

Solve the problem in two ways that make sense to you.

One way:	**Another way:**

There are _____ berries altogether.

Exploring Measurement

Measure Pascal's tongue using Rapunzel's paintbrush.

Pascal's tongue is 5 paintbrushes long.

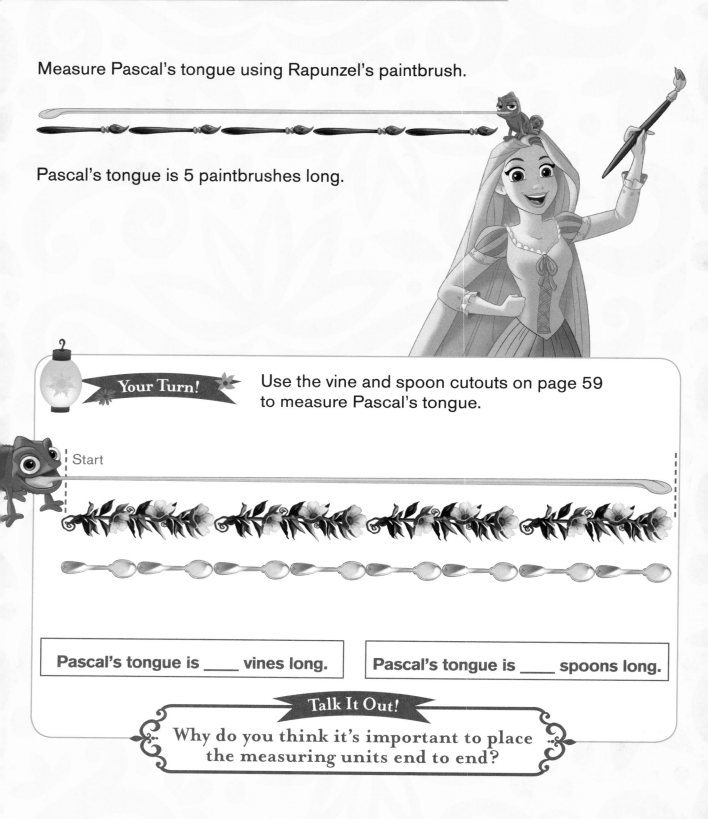

Your Turn! Use the vine and spoon cutouts on page 59 to measure Pascal's tongue.

Start

Pascal's tongue is ____ vines long.

Pascal's tongue is ____ spoons long.

Talk It Out!

Why do you think it's important to place the measuring units end to end?

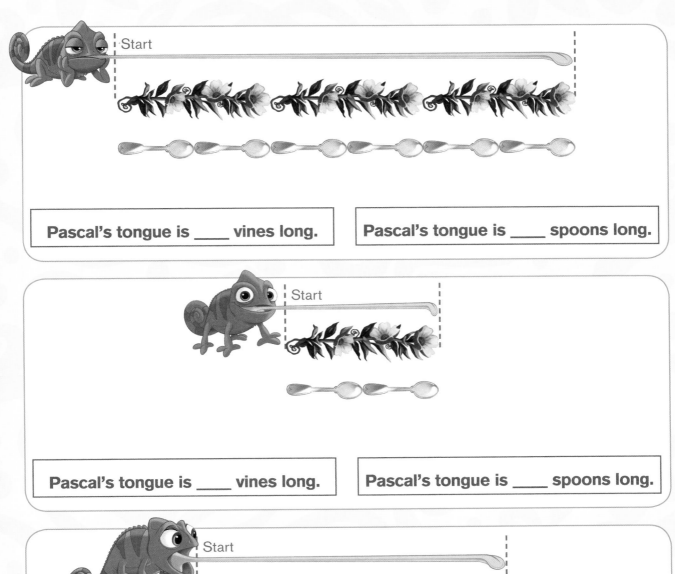

Pascal's tongue is ____ vines long.

Pascal's tongue is ____ spoons long.

Pascal's tongue is ____ vines long.

Pascal's tongue is ____ spoons long.

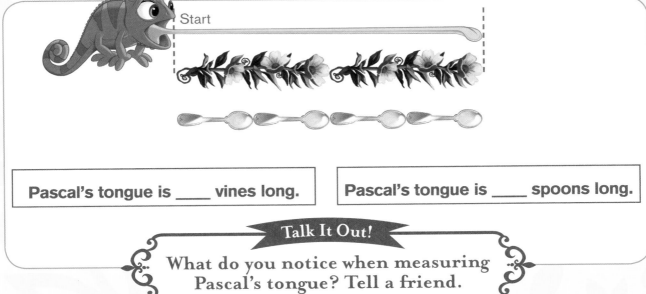

Pascal's tongue is ____ vines long.

Pascal's tongue is ____ spoons long.

Talk It Out!

What do you notice when measuring Pascal's tongue? Tell a friend.

Under the Sea Subtraction

Ariel has 16 forks.
She gives 7 to Flounder.
How many forks does Ariel have now?

One way:

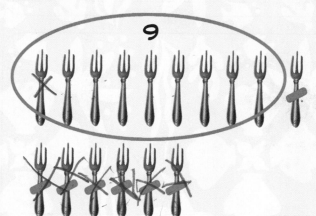

9

- Show 16.
- Cross out 7.
- Count what is left.
- The number left is the answer.

Another way:

0	1	2	3	4	5	6	7	8	9
10	11	12	13	14	15	16	17	18	19
20	21	22	23	24	25	26	27	28	29
30	31	32	33	34	35	36	37	38	39

- Start at 16.
- Count back 7 by ones.
- The number you land on is the answer.

Number sentence: 16 – 7 = 9
Ariel has 9 forks now.

Your Turn!

Solve this problem in two ways that make sense to you.

Ariel has 9 **forks.**

She gives 6 **to Flounder.**

How many forks does Ariel have now?

Choose a number set.

(9 6) | (99 36) (59 26) (29 16)

One way:

3

$$9 - 6 = 3$$

Another way:

0	1	2	3	4	5	6	7	8	9
10	11	12	13	14	15	16	17	18	19
20	21	22	23	24	25	26	27	28	29
30	31	32	33	34	35	36	37	38	39
40	41	42	43	44	45	46	47	48	49
50	51	52	53	54	55	56	57	58	59
60	61	62	63	64	65	66	67	68	69
70	71	72	73	74	75	76	77	78	79
80	81	82	83	84	85	86	87	88	89
90	91	92	93	94	95	96	97	98	99

Number sentence:

_____

Ariel has _____ forks now.

Open Number Sentences: Addition

There are 8 birds listening to Aurora sing.
Some are red and some are blue.
Color the birds to show different ways to make 8.

Write an equation to match each combination.

Birds	Equation
▽ ▽ ▽ ▽ ▽ ▽ ▽ ▽	
▽ ▽ ▽ ▽ ▽ ▽ ▽ ▽	
▽ ▽ ▽ ▽ ▽ ▽ ▽ ▽	
▽ ▽ ▽ ▽ ▽ ▽ ▽ ▽	
▽ ▽ ▽ ▽ ▽ ▽ ▽ ▽	
▽ ▽ ▽ ▽ ▽ ▽ ▽ ▽	
▽ ▽ ▽ ▽ ▽ ▽ ▽ ▽	
▽ ▽ ▽ ▽ ▽ ▽ ▽ ▽	
▽ ▽ ▽ ▽ ▽ ▽ ▽ ▽	

Talk It Out!

What do you notice
about the equations?

Aurora picked 10 strawberries.
Some were large and some were small.

Draw the strawberries to show
different ways to make 10.

Strawberries	Equation

Grouping by Hundreds, Tens, and Ones

Tiana is making a lot of beignets.
How many? Let's count.

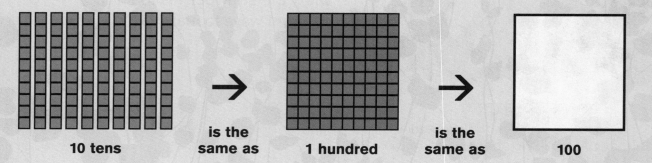

| 10 tens | is the same as | 1 hundred | is the same as | 100 |

One way: 145

| Hundreds | Tens | Ones |

Another way: 145

| Hundreds | Tens | Ones |

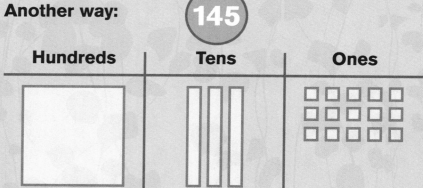

Your Turn! Build a number in two different ways.
Draw the hundreds, tens, and ones.

Pick one of these numbers to build:

124	253	365	492

Write it in the oval below.

$\bigcirc$

One way:

Hundreds	Tens	Ones

Another way:

Hundreds	Tens	Ones

Talk It Out!

Tell someone another way to make your
number with hundreds, tens, and ones.

Solving Problems with Addition and Subtraction

Mulan spots many lanterns in the Imperial City.
First she counts 14 orange lanterns.
Then she counts some green lanterns.
Altogether, Mulan counts 29 lanterns.
How many green lanterns did she count?

One way: Count on with an open number line.

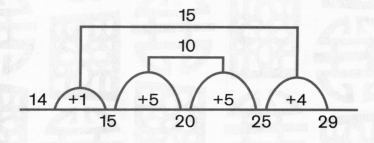

Find friendly numbers.

- **First, start at 14.**
- **Next, add 1 to get to the friendly number 15.**
- **Then add 5s to get to 25.**
- **Last, add 4 to get to 29.**

Another way: Count on with a 0–99 chart.

0	1	2	3	4	5	6	7	8	9
10	11	12	13	(14)	15	16	17	18	19
20	21	22	23	(24)	25	26	27	28	(29)
30	31	32	33	34	35	36	37	38	39

- **Start at 14**
- **Count on by ten and then ones until you reach 29.**

Number sentence: <u>14 + 15 = 29</u>
Mulan counts <u>15</u> green lanterns.

Your Turn!

Help Mulan solve this problem in two ways that make sense to you.

Mulan sees ⬚ **green kites.**

She also sees purple kites in the sky.

Mulan sees a total of ⬚ **green and purple kites.**

How many purple kites does Mulan see?

Choose a number set.

(52 97)   (12 37)   (32 67)   (22 47)

One way:

Another way:

0	1	2	3	4	5	6	7	8	9
10	11	12	13	14	15	16	17	18	19
20	21	22	23	24	25	26	27	28	29
30	31	32	33	34	35	36	37	38	39
40	41	42	43	44	45	46	47	48	49
50	51	52	53	54	55	56	57	58	59
60	61	62	63	64	65	66	67	68	69
70	71	72	73	74	75	76	77	78	79
80	81	82	83	84	85	86	87	88	89
90	91	92	93	94	95	96	97	98	99

Number sentence: _____

Mulan sees _____ purple kites.

Talk It Out!

What was tricky about
this problem? Why?

Exploring Patterns and Structure in Numbers

Cinderella hears many patterns in the music she plays.

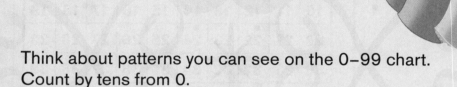

Word Bank

column	row	odd	even
tens place	ones place	digit	number

Think about patterns you can see on the 0–99 chart.
Count by tens from 0.
Color each number you count.
What happens?

0	1	2	3	4	5	6	7	8	9
10	11	12	13	14	15	16	17	18	19
20	21	22	23	24	25	26	27	28	29
30	31	32	33	34	35	36	37	38	39
40	41	42	43	44	45	46	47	48	49
50	51	52	53	54	55	56	57	58	59
60	61	62	63	64	65	66	67	68	69
70	71	72	73	74	75	76	77	78	79
80	81	82	83	84	85	86	87	88	89
90	91	92	93	94	95	96	97	98	99

What do you notice?

- **Each number has a 0 in the ones place.**
- **The digit in the tens place go up by one in each row.**

Color all the numbers
with a 4 in the ones place.

What do you notice?

0	1	2	3	4	5	6	7	8	9
10	11	12	13	14	15	16	17	18	19
20	21	22	23	24	25	26	27	28	29
30	31	32	33	34	35	36	37	38	39
40	41	42	43	44	45	46	47	48	49
50	51	52	53	54	55	56	57	58	59
60	61	62	63	64	65	66	67	68	69
70	71	72	73	74	75	76	77	78	79
80	81	82	83	84	85	86	87	88	89
90	91	92	93	94	95	96	97	98	99

0	1	2	3	4	5	6	7	8	9
10	11	12	13	14	15	16	17	18	19
20	21	22	23	24	25	26	27	28	29
30	31	32	33	34	35	36	37	38	39
40	41	42	43	44	45	46	47	48	49
50	51	52	53	54	55	56	57	58	59
60	61	62	63	64	65	66	67	68	69
70	71	72	73	74	75	76	77	78	79
80	81	82	83	84	85	86	87	88	89
90	91	92	93	94	95	96	97	98	99

Color all the even numbers.

Do you notice a pattern?

Count by fives from 0.
Color in the numbers.

**How are counting by fives
and tens similar? Why?**

0	1	2	3	4	5	6	7	8	9
10	11	12	13	14	15	16	17	18	19
20	21	22	23	24	25	26	27	28	29
30	31	32	33	34	35	36	37	38	39
40	41	42	43	44	45	46	47	48	49
50	51	52	53	54	55	56	57	58	59
60	61	62	63	64	65	66	67	68	69
70	71	72	73	74	75	76	77	78	79
80	81	82	83	84	85	86	87	88	89
90	91	92	93	94	95	96	97	98	99

Solving Problems with Addition and Subtraction

Merida has some arrows.
She gets 23 more for her quiver.
Now she has 49.
How many arrows did Merida have to start with?

One way:

$$\square + 23 = 49, \text{ so } 23 + \square = 49$$

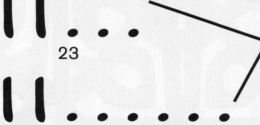

23

33 43 44 45 46 47 48 49

> **Number sentence:** 23 + (26) = 49
> Merida had 26 arrows to start with.

Another way:

$$\square + 23 = 49, \text{ so } 49 - 23 = \square$$

> **Number sentence:** 49 - 23 = (26)
> Merida had 26 arrows to start with.

Talk It Out!

Tell a friend how both addition and subtraction
can be used to solve this problem.

Solve this problem in two ways that make sense to you.

Merida has some arrows.

She gets **more for her quiver.**

Now Merida has **arrows.**

How many arrows did Merida have to start with?

Choose a number set.

(15 28)   (95 168)   (35 88)   (65 98)

One way:

Another way:

Number sentence: _____

Merida had _____ arrows to start with.

Which strategy made the most sense to you and why?

How Timely!

Belle thinks the best time is when it is time to read.
Let's learn about telling time.

The minute hand goes *fast*.
It is colored red to help you remember: red → fast.
The hour hand goes *slowly*.
It is colored blue to help you remember: blue → slow.

minute hand

hour hand

Analog Time ⟶

Digital Time ⟶ 3:00

Your Turn!

Write the digital time.

:

Draw the hour and minute hands to match the digital time.

8:00

Cogsworth knows all about time!
There are 60 minutes in an hour.
There are 30 minutes in a half hour.

Analog Time ⟶

The time is 10:30. | 10:30

Your Turn!

Write the digital time.

Draw the hour and minute hands to match the digital time.

:

9:30

Talk It Out!
What is important to remember when telling time to the half hour?

©Disney

Telling Time and Time Elapse

Mrs. Potts and Chip are making a special dinner.
They start at 2:00.
Dinner is served at 6:00.
How long did it take them to make dinner?

2:00

6:00

One way:

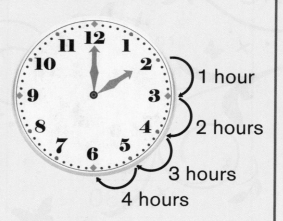

1 hour

2 hours

3 hours

4 hours

Another way:

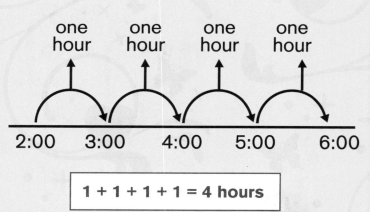

| one hour | one hour | one hour | one hour |

2:00   3:00   4:00   5:00   6:00

1 + 1 + 1 + 1 = 4 hours

It took <u>4</u> hours for Mrs. Potts and Chip to prepare dinner.

Your Turn!

Belle and the Beast are reading together.

They start reading at [   ] **.**

They finish reading at [   ] **.**

How long did Belle and the Beast read?

Choose a number set.

(3:00   10:00)   (8:00   3:00)   (2:00   11:00)

Use pictures, numbers, or words to solve in a way that makes sense to you.

One way:

| **Belle and the Beast read for _____ hours.** |

Another way:

| **Belle and the Beast read for _____ hours.** |

Solving Problems with Addition and Subtraction

Cinderella drew 45 sketches
for a new dress.
She kept the very best sketches
and threw away the rest.
Now she has 21 sketches.

How many sketches
did Cinderella throw away?

One way:

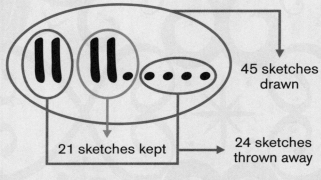

45 sketches
drawn

21 sketches kept

24 sketches
thrown away

- **Start with 45.**
- **Subtract the number of sketches Cinderella kept.**
- **The number left is the number she threw away.**

Another way:

Count up from sketches that are left.

$$21 + \square = 45$$

31 41 42 43 44 45

(24)

sketches
thrown away

- **Start with 21.**
- **Count by tens and then by ones to 45.**
- **The number you counted up is the answer.**

  21 + 24 = 45

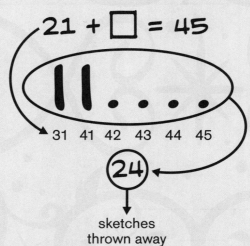

Your Turn! Solve this problem in two ways that make sense to you.

Gus picked up **kernels of corn.**

He ate some of the corn.

Now he has **kernels left.**

How many kernels of corn did Gus eat?

Choose a number set.

$$\boxed{89 \quad 35} \qquad \boxed{29 \quad 15} \qquad \boxed{179 \quad 65} \qquad \boxed{59 \quad 25}$$

Solve the problem using pictures, numbers, or words.
Use any strategy that makes sense to you.

One way:	**Another way:**

Number sentence: _____

Gus ate _____ kernels of corn.

Talk It Out!

Tell someone *why* you chose the strategy you chose.

©Disney

Grotto Graphs and Treasure Tallies

Ariel collected the treasures below and put them in her secret grotto.

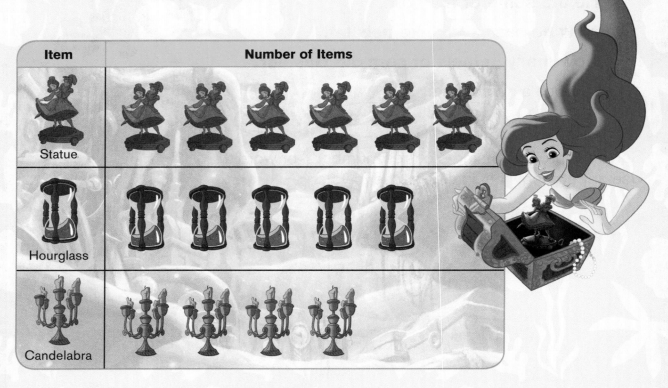

Item	Number of Items
Statue	(6 statues)
Hourglass	(5 hourglasses)
Candelabra	(4 candelabras)

Make a tally chart to match the pictograph above.

Item	Number of Items
Statue	卌 I
Hourglass	卌
Candelabra	IIII

- What does Ariel have the most of?
- What does Ariel have the least of?
- How many more statues does Ariel have than candelabras?

Your Turn!

Use the cutouts of Ariel's ocean friends on page 61 to create a pictograph below.

Ocean Animal	Number of Ocean Animals
Dolphin	
Crab	
Seahorse	

Now make a tally chart to match your pictograph.

Ocean Animal	Number of Ocean Animals
Dolphin	
Crab	
Seahorse	

Talk It Out!

Based on your tally chart, how many ocean friends does Ariel have altogether?

Fair Sharing

Merida gave Hamish, Hubert, and Harris 12 muffins.

They each got the same number of muffins.

How many muffins did each brother get?

One way:

Pass out like dealing cards.

1 2 3 4   1 2 3 4   1 2 3 4

Another way:

Pass out in pairs.

2   4   2   4   2   4

Hamish, Hubert, and Harris each got <u>4</u> muffins.

Solve this problem in two different ways that make sense to you.

Merida collected _____ **eggs.**

She gave Hamish, Hubert, and Harris all the eggs to crack open into a big bowl.

They each got the same number of eggs.

How many eggs did each of Merida's brothers get?

Choose a number.

 9   **15**   **27**   **36**

One way: **Another way:**

Hamish, Hubert, and Harris each got _____ eggs.

Talk It Out!

How did you make sure Hamish, Hubert, and Harris got the same number of eggs?

©Disney

Fair Sharing with Fractions

One Whole	One Half	One Fourth or One Quarter

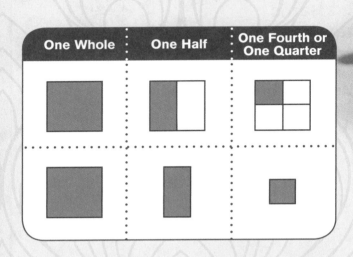

4 people share 6 cakes.
Each person gets the same amount.
How many cakes, including any parts, does each person get?

One way:

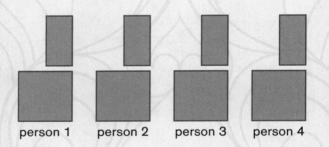

| person 1 | person 2 | person 3 | person 4 |

Each person gets 1 whole and 1 half.

Another way:

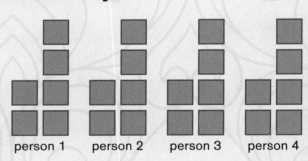

| person 1 | person 2 | person 3 | person 4 |

Each person gets 6 fourths or quarters.

Each person gets <u>one and a half</u> cakes.

Your Turn!

Solve this problem in two ways that make sense to you.

[____] **people share** [____] **crackers.**

How many crackers, including parts, does each person get?

Choose a number set.

One way: | **Another way:**

Each person gets _____ **crackers.**

Talk It Out!

Are two fourths the same as one half? How do you know?

Solving Problems with Addition and Subtraction

Pocahontas picked some ears of corn.
Meeko took 14 of them.
Now Pocahontas has 23 ears of corn left.
How many ears of corn did Pocahontas pick?

One way:

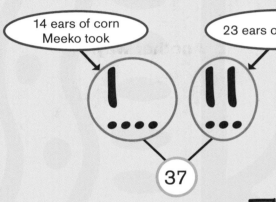

14 ears of corn Meeko took

23 ears of corn left

37

The number of ears of corn Meeko took plus the number of ears of corn left equals the total number of ears of corn Pocahontas picked.

$$\square - 14 = 23, \text{ so } 14 + 23 = \square$$

Another way:

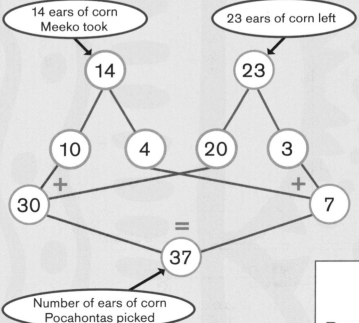

14 ears of corn Meeko took

23 ears of corn left

14

23

10   4   20   3

+   +

30   7

=

37

Number of ears of corn Pocahontas picked

Let's break the numbers down:

- First, break 14 and 23 down into tens and ones:
  14 = 10 + 4   23 = 20 + 3
- Then, add the ones:
  4 + 3 = 7
- Next, add the tens:
  10 + 20 = 30
- Last, add the tens and ones:
  30 + 7 = 37

Number sentence:
<u>14 + 23 = 37</u> so <u>37 - 14 = 23</u>
Pocahontas picked <u>37</u> ears of corn.

Your Turn! Solve this problem in two ways that make sense to you.

Pocahontas picked some ears of corn.

Meeko took _____ **of them.**

Now Pocahontas has _____ **ears of corn left.**

How many ears of corn did Pocahontas pick?

Choose a number set.

 117 78   37 28   17 18   147 98

One way: **Another way:**

Number sentence: _____

Pocahontas picked _____ ears of corn.

Talk It Out!

What tip would you give a friend who had to solve this problem?

Shaping Up

Some of the paintings Rapunzel creates
have lots of shapes.

Glossary of Plane Shapes					
Shape	Square	Rectangle	Triangle	Circle	Hexagon
Picture	■	▬	▲	●	⬡
Number of Sides	4	4	3	0	6

You can *compose* new shapes using smaller shapes.
These are called *composite* shapes.
Shapes can have the same number of sides but look different.

Rapunzel is making a mosaic using only squares.
Help her create different designs.

Use 4 squares to compose a mosaic.
   Rule #1: The SIDES must completely touch.
   Rule #2: The composite shapes must be different.

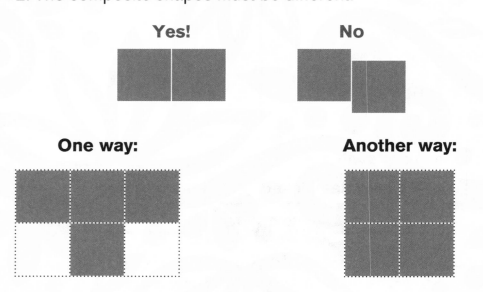

Yes!   **No**

One way: **Another way:**

Use the square cutouts on page 61.
Make new shapes with 4 squares each.

Trace your shapes on the grid below. Reuse the squares.

 Helpful Tip!

Test that your shapes are <u>different</u> by flipping, sliding, and turning them.

flip

slide

turn

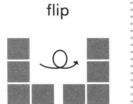

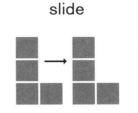

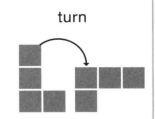

You can *compose* new shapes
using smaller shapes.
These composite shapes may have
the same number of sides,
but still look different.

Use the triangle cutouts on page 61.
Make new shapes using 5 triangles each.
How many different shapes can you make with 5 triangles?

Rule #1: The SIDES must completely touch.
Rule #2: The composite shapes must be different.

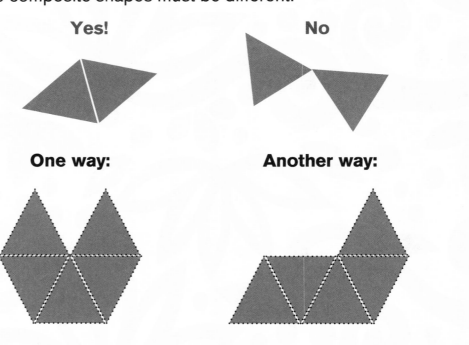

Test that your shapes
are <u>different</u> by
flipping, sliding,
and turning them.

flip

slide

turn

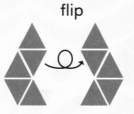
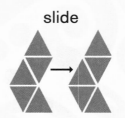
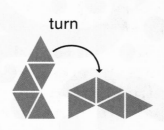

Use the triangle cutouts on page 61. How many different shapes can you make with 5 triangles?

Trace your shapes on the grid below. Reuse the triangles.

Talk It Out!

Count the number of sides on the new composite shapes you made with squares and triangles. What did you find?

Geometric Gems

The gems the Dwarfs mine are solid figures.

Cube	Rectangular Prism	Square Pyramid	Sphere	Triangular Pyramid

You can compose solid (or three-dimensional) shapes
using plane (or two-dimensional) shapes.

Cubes are composed of squares.

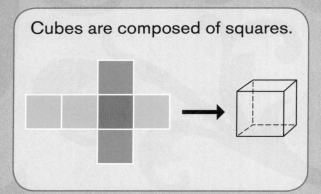

Square pyramids are composed
of squares and triangles.

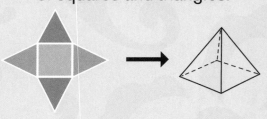

Rectangular
prisms are
composed of
squares and/or
rectangles.

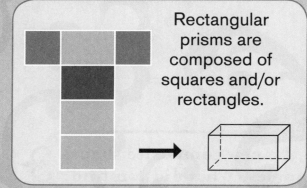

Triangular pyramids are
composed of triangles.

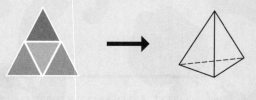

Your Turn! Use the net cutouts on page 63. Use scissors, tape, and an adult helper to make the gems.

Use the gems to create a tower on the space below. What do you notice?

Talk It Out!

Discuss the shapes you see as you create the solid figures. Which shapes do you think will work best for the gem tower? Why?

PAGE 5

Answers may vary for letters and numbers. Possibilities include:

Letters: A B C C A B C C

Numbers: 1 2 3 3 1 2 3 3

Actions: Answers will vary.

My Pattern Unit: Answers will vary.

PAGES 6-7

The order of numbers in the equations may vary.

Birds	Equation
	5 + 0 = 5
	4 + 1 = 5
	3 + 2 = 5
	2 + 3 = 5
	1 + 4 = 5
	0 + 5 = 5

The order of numbers in the equations may vary.

Rabbits	Equation
	7 + 0 = 7
	6 + 1 = 7
	5 + 2 = 7
	4 + 3 = 7
	3 + 4 = 7
	2 + 5 = 7
	1 + 6 = 7
	0 + 7 = 7

PAGE 9

42 is the same as 4 tens and 2 ones.

Tens	42	Ones

73 is the same as 7 tens and 3 ones.

Tens	73	Ones

PAGE 11

44:

Answers may vary. Possibilities include:

44 is the same as:

- 4 tens and 4 ones
- 3 tens and 14 ones
- 2 tens and 24 ones

35:

Answers may vary. Possibilities include:

35 is the same as:

- 3 tens and 5 ones
- 2 tens and 15 ones
- 1 ten and 25 ones

PAGES 12-13

Answers may vary.

PAGE 15

Strategies used will vary.

Solutions listed below according to number set selected.

(22; 23): 45

(42; 53): 95

(12; 13): 25

(72; 63): 135

PAGE 17

Answers may vary.

PAGE 19

Strategies used will vary.

Solutions listed below according to number set selected.

(4; 5): 20

(8; 2): 16

(6; 10): 60

(3; 4): 12

PAGES 20-21

1. Pascal's tongue is 4 vines long and 8 spoons long.
2. Pascal's tongue is 3 vines long and 6 spoons long.
3. Pascal's tongue is 1 vine long and 2 spoons long.
4. Pascal's tongue is 2 vines long and 4 spoons long.

Solutions listed below according to number set selected.

(9; 6): 3

(99; 36): 63

(59; 26): 33

(29; 16): 13

The order of numbers in the equations may vary.

Birds	Equation
●●●●●●●●	8 + 0 = 8
●●●●●●●●	7 + 1 = 8
●●●●●●●●	6 + 2 = 8
●●●●●●●●	5 + 3 = 8
●●●●●●●●	4 + 4 = 8
●●●●●●●●	3 + 5 = 8
●●●●●●●●	2 + 6 = 8
●●●●●●●●	1 + 7 = 8
●●●●●●●●	0 + 8 = 8

The order of numbers in the equations may vary.

Strawberries	Equation
🍓🍓🍓🍓🍓🍓🍓🍓🍓🍓	10 + 0 = 10
🍓🍓🍓🍓🍓🍓🍓🍓🍓🍓	9 + 1 = 10
🍓🍓🍓🍓🍓🍓🍓🍓🍓🍓	8 + 2 = 10
🍓🍓🍓🍓🍓🍓🍓🍓🍓🍓	7 + 3 = 10
🍓🍓🍓🍓🍓🍓🍓🍓🍓🍓	6 + 4 = 10
🍓🍓🍓🍓🍓🍓🍓🍓🍓🍓	5 + 5 = 10
🍓🍓🍓🍓🍓🍓🍓🍓🍓🍓	4 + 6 = 10
🍓🍓🍓🍓🍓🍓🍓🍓🍓🍓	3 + 7 = 10
🍓🍓🍓🍓🍓🍓🍓🍓🍓🍓	2 + 8 = 10
🍓🍓🍓🍓🍓🍓🍓🍓🍓🍓	1 + 9 = 10
🍓🍓🍓🍓🍓🍓🍓🍓🍓🍓	0 + 10 = 10

Answers may vary.

Solutions listed below according to number selected.

124 is the same as:

- 1 hundred, 2 tens, and 4 ones
- 0 hundreds, 11 tens, and 14 ones
- 0 hundreds, 10 tens, and 24 ones, and so on

253 is the same as:

- 2 hundreds, 5 tens, and 3 ones
- 1 hundred, 15 tens, and 3 ones
- 1 hundred, 14 tens, and 13 ones, and so on.

365 is the same as:

- 3 hundreds, 6 tens, and 5 ones
- 2 hundreds, 16 tens, and 5 ones
- 2 hundreds, 15 tens, and 15 ones, and so on.

492 is the same as:

- 4 hundreds, 9 tens, and 2 ones
- 3 hundreds, 19 tens, and 2 ones
- 3 hundreds, 18 tens, and 12 ones, and so on.

Strategies used will vary.

Solutions listed below according to number set selected.

(52; 97): 45

(12; 37): 25

(32; 67): 35

(22; 47): 25

Numbers with a 4
in the ones place

0	1	2	3	4	5	6	7	8	9
10	11	12	13	14	15	16	17	18	19
20	21	22	23	24	25	26	27	28	29
30	31	32	33	34	35	36	37	38	39
40	41	42	43	44	45	46	47	48	49
50	51	52	53	54	55	56	57	58	59
60	61	62	63	64	65	66	67	68	69
70	71	72	73	74	75	76	77	78	79
80	81	82	83	84	85	86	87	88	89
90	91	92	93	94	95	96	97	98	99

Even Numbers

0	1	2	3	4	5	6	7	8	9
10	11	12	13	14	15	16	17	18	19
20	21	22	23	24	25	26	27	28	29
30	31	32	33	34	35	36	37	38	39
40	41	42	43	44	45	46	47	48	49
50	51	52	53	54	55	56	57	58	59
60	61	62	63	64	65	66	67	68	69
70	71	72	73	74	75	76	77	78	79
80	81	82	83	84	85	86	87	88	89
90	91	92	93	94	95	96	97	98	99

Counting by 5s

0	1	2	3	4	5	6	7	8	9
10	11	12	13	14	15	16	17	18	19
20	21	22	23	24	25	26	27	28	29
30	31	32	33	34	35	36	37	38	39
40	41	42	43	44	45	46	47	48	49
50	51	52	53	54	55	56	57	58	59
60	61	62	63	64	65	66	67	68	69
70	71	72	73	74	75	76	77	78	79
80	81	82	83	84	85	86	87	88	89
90	91	92	93	94	95	96	97	98	99

PAGE 33

Strategies used will vary.
Solutions listed below according to number set selected.
(15; 28): 13
(95; 168): 73
(35; 88): 53

(65; 98): 33

PAGE 34

5:00

8:00

PAGE 35

3:30

9:30

PAGE 37

Strategies used will vary.
Solutions listed below according to number set selected.
(3:00; 10:00): 7 hours
(8:00; 3:00): 7 hours
(2:00; 11:00): 9 hours

PAGE 39

Strategies used will vary.
Solutions listed below according to number set selected.
(89; 35): 54
(29; 15): 14
(179; 65): 114
(59; 25): 34

PAGE 41

Answers will vary.
Tally marks in tally charts should match pictures in pictograph.

PAGE 43

Strategies used will vary.
Solutions listed below according to number selected.
(9): 3
(15): 5
(27): 9
(36): 12

PAGE 45

Strategies used will vary.
Solutions listed below according to number set selected.
(2; 7): 3 and one half
(2; 13): 6 and one half
(4; 22): 5 and one half
(4; 10): 2 and one half
(4; 18): 4 and one half
(2; 5): 2 and one half

PAGE 47

Strategies used will vary.
Solutions listed below according to number set selected.
(117; 78): 195
(37; 28): 65
(17; 18): 35
(147; 98): 245

PAGE 49

Answers will vary. Possibilities may include:

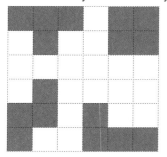

PAGE 51

Answers will vary. Possibilities may include:

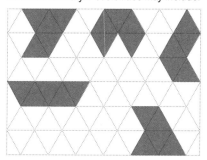

Cut It Out

Have an adult help you cut these components out to complete the lessons.

PAGE 5

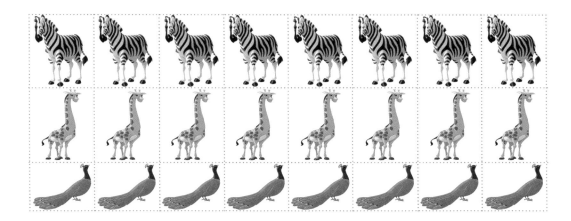

PAGE 9

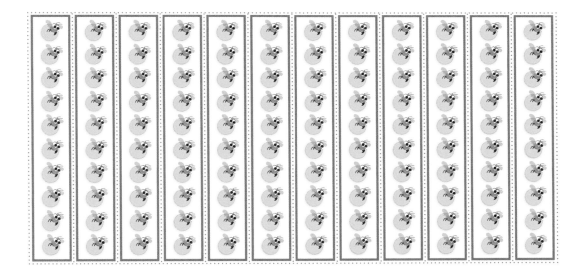

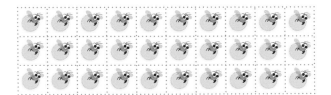

PAGES 10-11

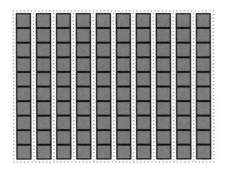
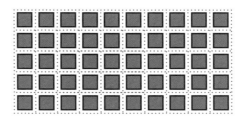

PAGES 20-21

PAGE 41

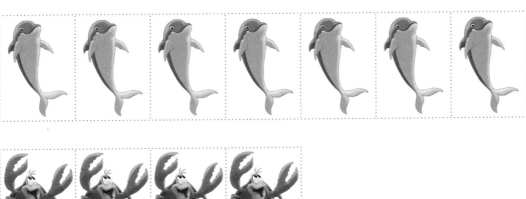

PAGE 49

PAGE 51

Use an adult helper, scissors, and tape to assemble the solid shapes.
Cut on the black dotted lines and fold on the white dashed lines.

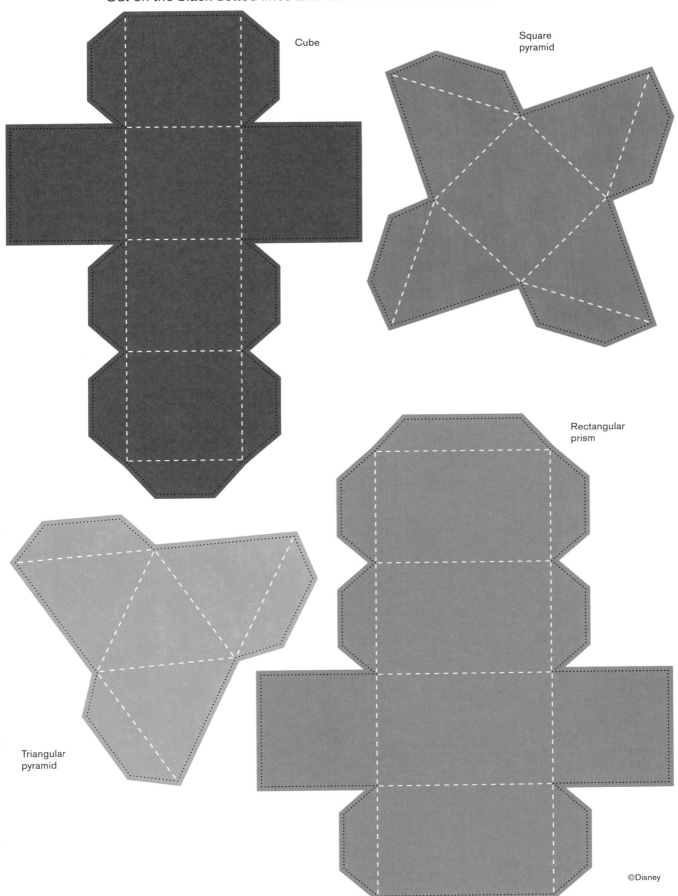

Cube

Square pyramid

Rectangular prism

Triangular pyramid

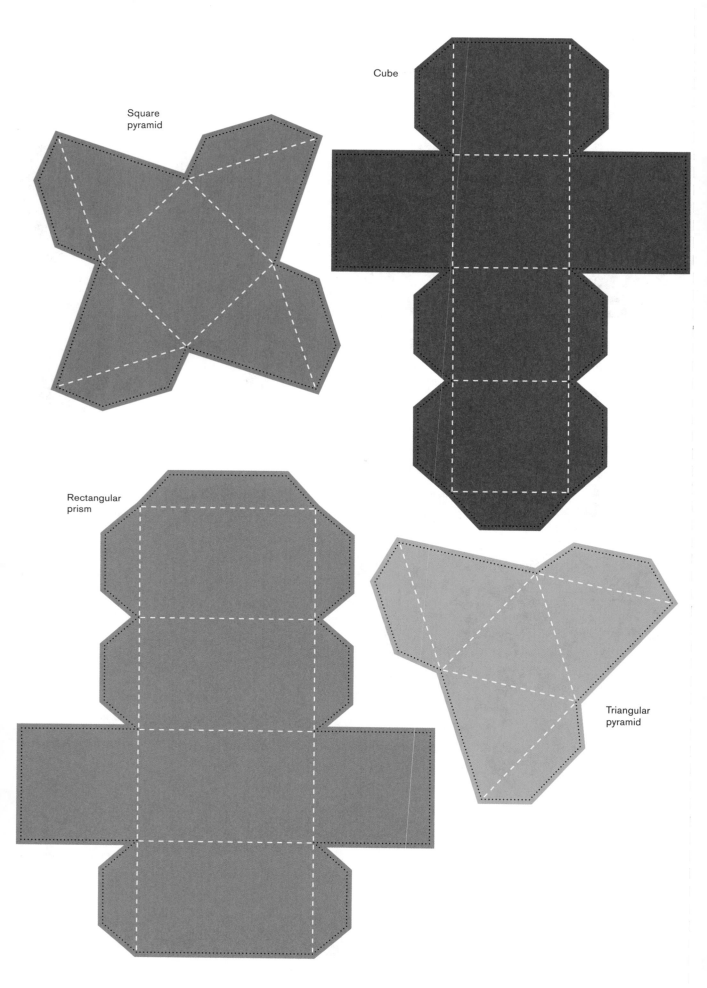

Square pyramid

Cube

Rectangular prism

Triangular pyramid

Additional Work Space

Additional Work Space